D0504348

# KATE & WILLS
# UP THE AISLE

The photographs in this book do not, nor are they intended to, represent any actual event that has taken place, nor that will take place. The well-known individuals depicted in this book are portrayed using lookalikes. These well-known individuals have not had any involvement in the creation of the photographs in this book and they have not approved, nor has their approval been sought for, the publication of these photographs.

Quadrille
PUBLISHING

# KATE & WILLS
# UP THE AISLE

## ALISON JACKSON

Words by Kitty Soames

*A Right Royal Fairy Tale*

$\mathcal{O}$nce upon a time a prince and princess had a beautiful baby boy. They called him William. But there was a naughty fairy at their wedding and she bewitched the prince. Caught in her spell, he left his winsome princess and married that fairy.

$\mathcal{T}$he young Prince William decided that his own wedding, one day, would be very different – a true fairytale.

*N*ot so far away – and yet, in another world – a very different couple had wed.

*T*hey were humble, yet happy. Carole Goldsmith had been born a poor maiden, but one whose great beauty was famed throughout her native Norwood. She dreamed of a magic carpet that would whisk her out of the council flat into which she had been born, and to a life of jumbo jets, castles and cake. Her glamour was such that she was summoned by British Airways to be a trolley dolly. There she met her handsome prince – Michael Middleton. This fine Yorkshireman, son of a pilot, was a flight despatcher and he immediately took the curvaceous Carole under his wing.

$\mathcal{A}$ few months before the young Prince William was born, Michael and Carole were blessed with the birth of a daughter. Her hair was as black as ebony, her skin as white as snow, though she had a cheeky round face. They named her Catherine Elizabeth, a truly regal name for a baby who had been naturally given all the graces of the kingdom: she was fair of face, fit of body, and clever enough to get into St. Andrew's University to read History of Art at the critical moment.

$\mathcal{C}$arole lived in a small house in Berkshire, but she dreamt big dreams. She worked night and day filling party bags to sell to richer mothers and at last, when the young Catherine was seven, Carole had sold enough of them to send her and her little sister and brother to private prep school. The first, tiny steps towards Buckingham Palace had been taken! And from St. Andrew's School in Pangbourne came the dizzying leap towards one of England's oldest and finest public schools, Marlborough College. Motto – 'Deus Dat Incrementum' – God Giveth the Increase'. In Kate's case, he certainly would. There she showed promise in acting, in sport, and in general fanciability, all of which earned her the nickname 'Princess in Waiting.'

She did not have to wait long.
On the rocky outcrops of St. Andrew's
University on the coast of Scotland,
buffeted by the North Sea, she was to
meet her Prince.

$\mathcal{W}$illiam, by now a handsome
young buck, keen to taste the freedoms
of university life after long years
incarcerated in a tailcoat at Eton, fell for
the raven-haired siren. Her charms first
ensnared him in a see-through dress on
a catwalk.

*S*oon they were an item and she was taking him home to Bucklebury, Berks, to meet the family. Here there were no liveried servants, no family portraits, no throne room. Not even a moat. And yet... William found there was something more valuable than any of those. The house had Heart. The Middletons welcomed the young Prince into their home as if he were one of their own.

→1A        2        →2A        3        →3A
CR-36        8        FUJI        9        100 ACRO

→7A        8        →8A        9        →9A
0 ACROS        14        744        15        ACR-36

→13A        14        →14A        15        →15A
0 ACROS        14        744        15        ACR-36

*H*ow could the young Kate not day-dream of
gilded future with her handsome prince at her
le? Would she be the one who would
e day be Queen?

*T*he romance blossomed in private,
far from the prying eyes of the world,
including *Heat, Hello, OK!* and their
pesky ilk.

*P*ushed cruelly into the real world after their Scottish idyll, William joined the army and Kate....Kate....Well, how could any job match up to the one she longed for? Being a part-time accessories buyer at Jigsaw just couldn't quite cut it.

$\mathcal{H}$er prince had become an officer.
But was he a gentleman?

$\mathscr{D}$ark clouds were gathering over the romance.
There was a big bad wolf waiting around the
corner, and his name was Commitmentphobia.

One dreadful day, William called time on the love affair down a crackly mobile phone line. He plunged into a maelstrom of blowsy blondes, treasure chest cocktails and champagne at Mahiki. She wept at home in Bucklebury. But one glass of white wine and half a tub of Ben and Jerry's later, Carole cracked the whip and told her it was time for action, not self-pity.

*It* was a call to arms. There were three tasks, said Carole. She must have a lustworthy body. She must have a peerless face. And she must cook better than any Palace chef.

*N*ot for the first time, or the last, Carole was right. It worked. Joy unbounded! Love was rekindled, and the happy couple moved to Anglesey in North Wales, where William was flying his chopper. There they discovered blissful domesticity.

$\mathcal{P}$rince William had always had a thing about Africa. So he took his one true love to the slopes of Mount Kenya to stay in a hut on an estate belonging to an ex-girlfriend. Alone at last, they plighted their troth. In Africa, she agreed to become his Queen.

$\mathcal{G}$reat rejoicing broke out throughout
Bucklebury. Carole had won!
Over at Highgrove, Charles and Camilla
sulked at reports that the nation chose
Wills and Kate for King and Queen
ahead of them.

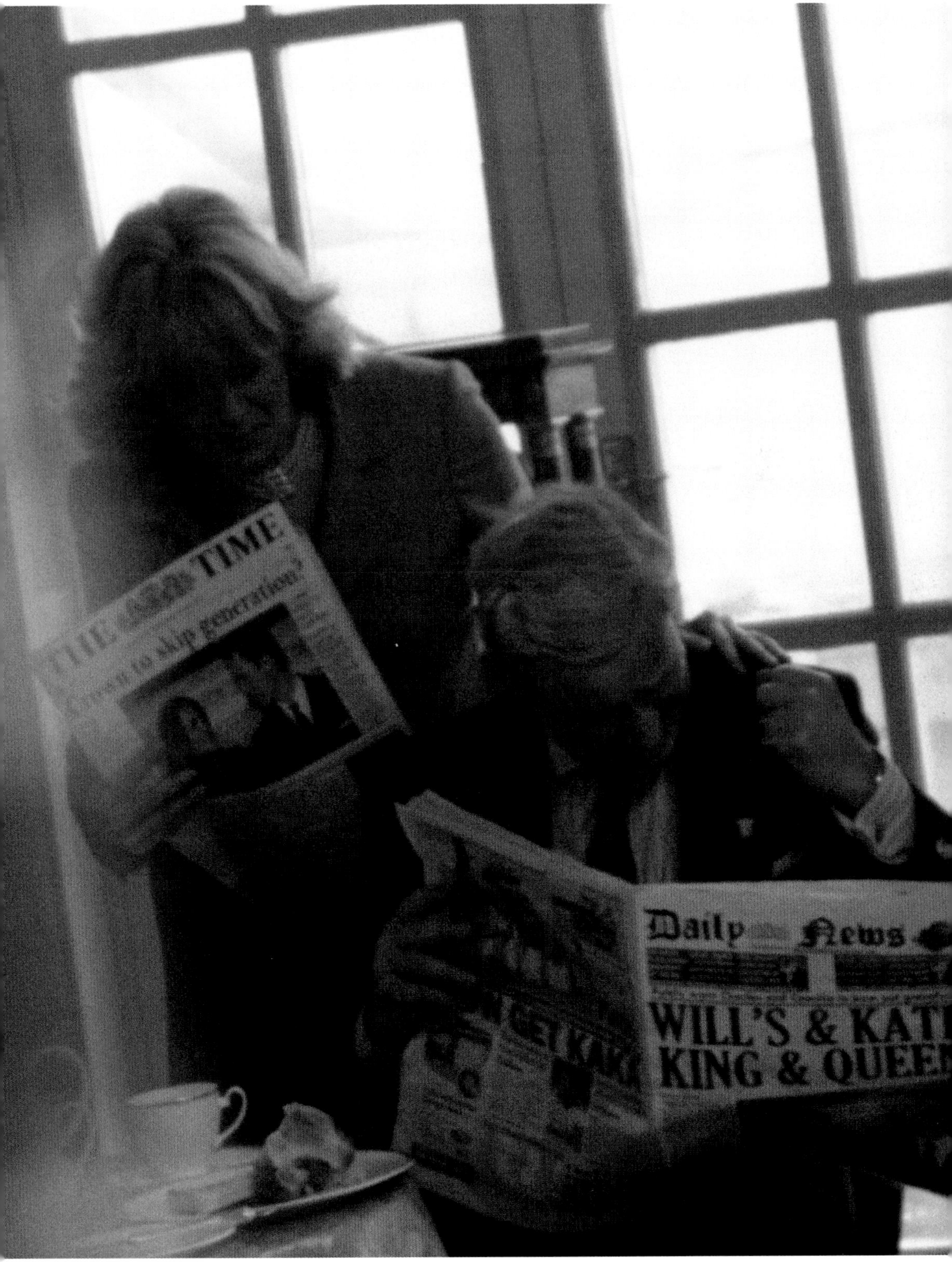
TIME
skip generation?
Daily News
WILL'S & KAT
KING & QUEE

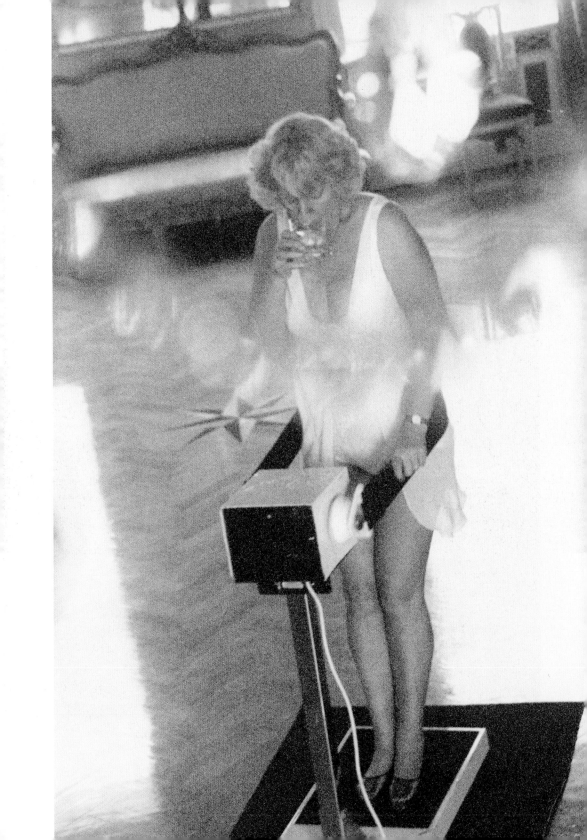

A                    2          →2A          3          →3F
-36                  8          FUJI         9          100 A

A                    8          →8A          9          →9A
ACROS                14         744          15         ACR-

BA                   14         →14A         15         →15
ACROS                14         744          15         ACR-

At last, the Queen introduced Kate into
the circle of trust. She met the corgis, and
Her Majesty even showed her how to
break a pheasant's neck with one hand.

𝒯here were lessons to learn. Coats of arms to be commissioned. Bridesmaids and pages to choose, finger buffets to select. And above all, the dress.

*H*er friends organised the greatest and
most secretive hen party that had ever
been held in the land. What happened
there, stays there.

$\mathscr{S}$he realized she had a lot to learn. But she
was willing to be taught by the experts.

𝓜eanwhile, William's naughty little brother, the dashing Prince Harry, gathered the royal crew for one final thrash. It had to beat all the other nights out, and that was a tall order. But he managed it. And the police files have been destroyed.

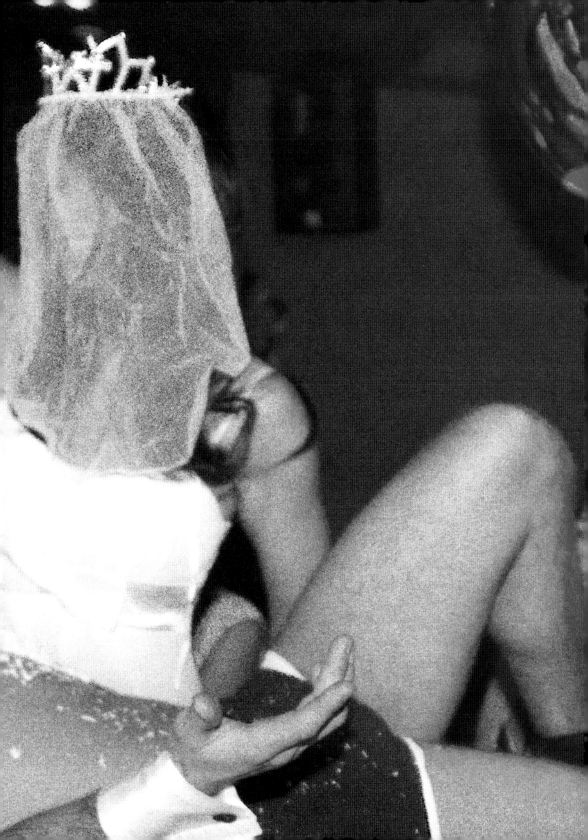

*It* takes a lot to make Carole nervous,
but meeting the Queen did require a bit
of private practice.

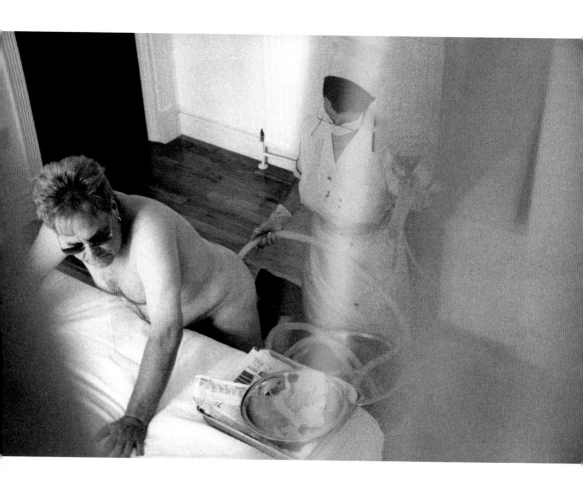

$\mathcal{A}$s preparations for the wedding gathered pace, everyone prayed that they might be asked to take part in some way. Some came bearing instruments hoping to perform – the Throne Room turned into a Royal version of *Britain's Got Talent*. Some just waited by the letterbox for a great big stiffie.

*O*thers were more proactive, reminding
the Royals of their good nature and years
of friendship.

The Queen had her views on who
should come. Banished was the unbridled
redhead who had once wormed her
unworthy way into the monarch's
affections.
In came that thrusting young Prime
Minister who'd been at prep school
with Prince Edward. If only she could
remember his name.

The finest dressmakers in Christendom competed with lengths of tulle and bolts of shimmering silk to make the gown. Would it be Issa? Would it be Bruce? Certainly not that nasty, knickerless old crone Dame Vivienne, who'd snapped under the pressure and accused the bride of having no style. Out!

*Finally*, the great day dawned. Friday, April 29ᵗʰ, 2011. With millions of loyal subjects lining the streets of London waving the Union Jacks that they'd bought from the Middletons' Party Pieces website, street parties kicking off throughout the kingdom and a billion more watching on televisions all over the globe, the perfect Princess arrived in a car, though she was to leave in a carriage.

*As* Kate mounted the steps of Westminster Abbey, at five minutes past eleven o'clock, all 1900 guests gasped at her loveliness and most – all but the hardest-hearted – shed a tear. Her little sister Pippa looked foxy and the ushers were smitten. Two pages and four bridesmaids – some unfeasibly young – had been bribed with crisps by their hysterical parents.

*Prince* William, now almost recovered from his epic stag do, swayed gently by the altar. As ever, Prince Harry wasn't much help. Their old nanny Tiggy was looking sternly at William from a pew. He must pull himself together and remember to say all his middle names in the right order. Arthur Philip Louis..or was it Louis Philip Arthur…?

*P*rince Harry knew that every single hot blonde in that Abbey was his for the asking that day. And he was right.

𝒜fter the Abbey, the Royal couple got
rid of the 1300 guests they didn't know
and went back to Buckingham Palace
for lunch for six hundred of their nearest
and dearest. It was the first buffet in
Royal Wedding history, and the foodstuffs
had been presented from far and wide,
though they were organic where possible.

Kate – or Catherine as she was now known – had not been looking forward to Harry's speech, and she was right. But not even the long list of ex-girlfriends, most of whom were listening, could dampen her spirits. She was a Princess at last, and the Royal Prince was hers, and hers alone.

The Prince and Princess danced all night, and the guests, and the
global television audience, had no doubt that they'd live happily ever after.

## ACKNOWLEDGEMENTS

I am incredibly indebted to all the people who have helped during the making of this book, for working so fast, under extreme pressure of time, yet with so much attention to detail.

Thanks to my publisher Quadrille for their help in turning this idea of mine into a reality. To Simon Davis for being such an understanding editor and for being so very helpful and to Helen Lewis, Anne Furniss and Lawrence for their encouragement, support and expertise. Thanks also to my agent Jonny Geller and Nick Marston from Curtis Brown.

Many thanks are due to Tom Rawstorne for his essential and continued creative input and editorial support. Without him and his ideas for the photographs this book would not be complete.

Thanks to George Bright for his brilliant ideas about the royals. Thanks to Andy Tapper, the brilliant post-production art director who helped to create the style of the book, and for his tireless retouching and editing down of the thousands of pictures I took over the course of this project.  Thanks to Andrew Farrar for his editing and retouching and to Jenny Dale for making sure that Wills looks like Wills! Thanks to my production team of Alicia Jones, Hannah Lane, Gustaf Manhem, Paul Desira and Kwesi Kwesi – who had to work quickly over the weekends and at night – and to the excellent design and art direction team of Jonathan Houghton Van Beek, Charlotte Copeland and Melissa Aldrate for their incredible styling and hard work. Thanks to Julian Small, Robert Radmall and Marie Amsolom, my camera assistants, for keeping me on track artistically and technically and for ordering my thousands of shots – I shot over 100,000 images for this work, so no small task – and to Sascha Ramin for keeping it all technically arranged and stored. Thanks to the skill of my hair and make-up and costume teams: Juliette Argent, Rebecca Wordingham, Jojo Copeland and Jennifer Davies, Lenka Padysakova and Johanne Bertaux. Thanks to Susan Scott and Nicci Topping for all their casting help, and to Ana Vav at Limelight people and Venette Shantelle at edge models for supplying excellent extras whose performances were amazing as always. Thanks also to Patrick Maxwell for editing the video and to Caroline Bridges and Rachael James on camera. And to Caroline Kellett for her great ideas.

And, of course, a big thank-you to all the lookalikes.

**Special thanks to:** Johanna Hehir (www.johanna-hehir.co.uk) for the fantastic wedding dresses; particularly Caroline Crompton and her great styling.  Mo Nabbach at M and M Hair Academy (www.mandmhairacademy.com); Tobyn Cleeves from Bell Tent (www.belltent.co.uk) Paul Allen from Thurloe's (www.thurloes.com); Mike and Anthony Woodley at Aces High, Dunsfold Aerodrome; The White House, Ealing (royal location); The Cranley Hotel, Surrey (www.thecranleyhotel.co.uk); Sixteen Hotel, The Firmdale Group, 16 Sumner Place, London SW7 3EG.

*Editorial director* Anne Furniss
*Creative director* Helen Lewis
*Project editor* Simon Davis
*Production director* Vincent Smith
*Production controller* James Finan

First published in 2011
by Quadrille Publishing Limited,
Alhambra House, 27–31 Charing Cross Road,
London WC2H 0LS
www.quadrille.co.uk

Photographs and text © Alison Jackson
Design and layout © 2011 Quadrille Publishing Limited

All rights reserved. No part of this book may
be reproduced, stored in a retrieval system
or transmitted in any form or by any means,
electronic, electrostatic, magnetic tape, mechanical,
photocopying, recording or otherwise, without the
prior permission in writing of the publisher.

Cataloguing in Publication Data: a catalogue
record for this book is available from the British
Library.

ISBN 978 184949 013 9

Printed in Spain